To _____

From _____

. . . because you deserve it!

THANK A TEACHER

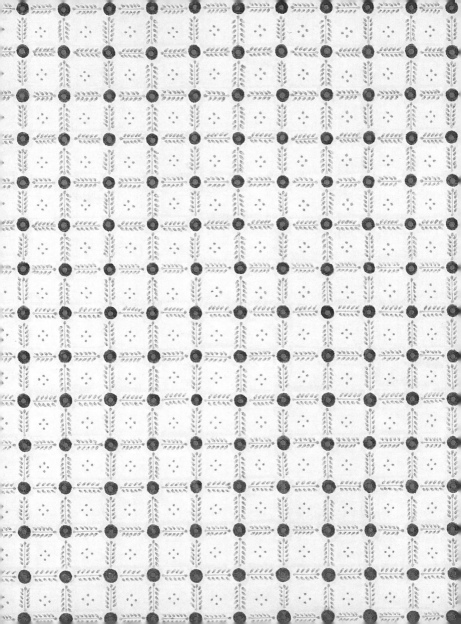

Thank a Teacher

Illustrated by
Mary Engelbreit

Andrews McMeel
Publishing

Kansas City

is a registered trademark of Mary Engelbreit Enterprises, Inc.

10 9 8 7 6 5 4 3 2 1

ISBN: 0-8362-5266-7

Written by Jan Miller Girando

Thank a Teacher

If each educated creature
took the time to thank a teacher
(even those who taught the lessons
of hard knocks),
whether mister, miss, or missus,
we'd applaud their "that's"
and "this's."
Without teachers, we would all be
dumb as rocks!

CREATING, ACTING, CHANGING

THAT is ETERNAL JOY

- Le Corbusier -

They have worth
beyond all measures,
Whether trained or simply treasures,
and it makes no difference
if they're young or old,
bold and forceful, kind and gentle,
witty, warm, and sentimental,
gruff and grouchy
with a tender heart of gold!

And a classroom isn't needed —
a true teacher's not impeded
if surroundings aren't exactly
up to par ...

A GOOD WORD IS LIKE A GOOD TREE WHOSE ROOT IS FIRMLY FIXED AND WHOSE TOP IS IN THE SKY. —THE KORAN

... for the secret of good coaching
is quite simply in approaching
every student as a bright
and rising star.

Teachers teach that limitations
are just minor aggravations.
We can make our dreams
reality someday!

The Girls

If we think that we can do it,
Then there's really nothing to it!
If it's in our heart,
there's nothing in our way!

Through example and instruction,
teachers offer introduction
to a galaxy of worlds
we've never seen.
New adventures are inviting!
Exploration seems exciting!
We can write a book or find
a new vaccine!

THERE IS ALWAYS ONE MOMENT IN CHILDHOOD WHEN THE DOOR OPENS AND LETS THE FUTURE IN.

—GRAHAM GREENE

We can learn to juggle numbers,
paint with golds and
reds and umbers,
argue courtroom law or
fix a car — voila! —
sell insurance, make a table,
run a restaurant, hook up cable,
give a speech or play an
instrument — Ta-dah!

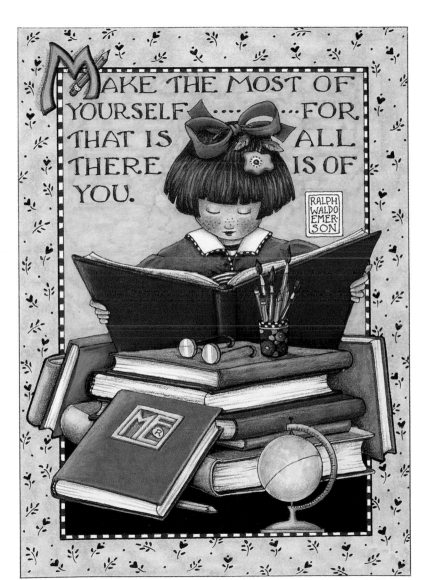

But there's more to education
than a classroom situation;
all our lessons aren't the ones
we learn in school.

There are teachers all around us
who cajole us, guide and hound us
to learn manners
and obey the golden rule!

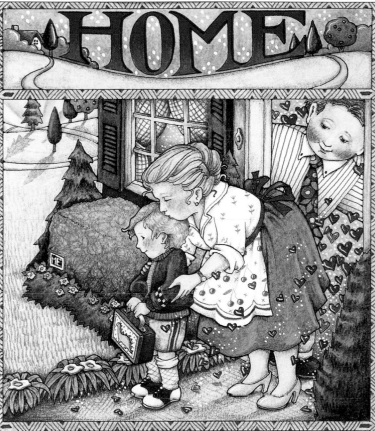

HOME

IS WHERE ONE STARTS FROM

······T.S. ELIOT·······

Our horizons are expanded
as we learn that underhanded
and untruthful methods
simply aren't correct.
When a circumstance gets sticky,
or temptation makes us tricky,
being honest helps regain
our self-respect.

Then one day, without our knowing,
we find out our smarts are showing
as we pass them on to
someone else in need,
and we see the light of learning
gaining strength and brightly burning
in another who is
following *our* lead.

If you have knowledge, let others light their candles by it.

So the circle is completed,
for the teaching is repeated.
We've begun to write
a new scenario,
and we thank with warm affection
those who fostered our perfection!
They mean more to us
than they will ever know.

MISS SMARTY

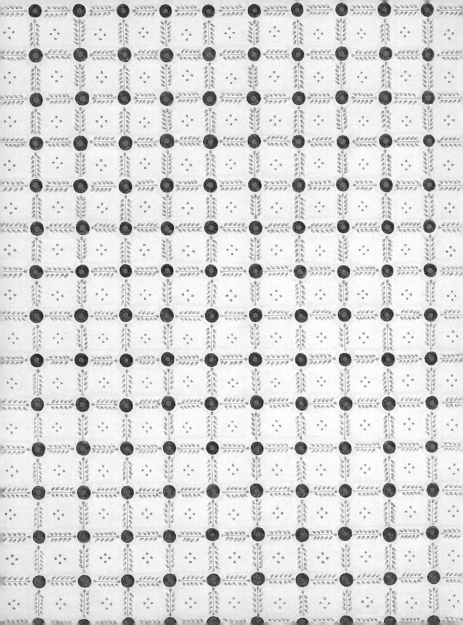